First edition for the United States and Canada published
in 2012 by Barron's Educational Series, Inc.

First published in 2012 by Wayland,
Hachette Children's Books,
338, Euston Rd., London NW1 3BH

Concept design: Kate Buxton
Series design: Paul Cherrill
All rights reserved.

All inquiries should be addressed to:
Barron's Educational Series, Inc.
250 Wireless Boulevard
Hauppauge, New York 11788
www.barronseduc.com

ISBN: 978-1-4380-0187-6

Library of Congress Control No. 2012940639

Printed in China

Manufactured by: Shenzhen Wing King Tong Paper Products Co. Ltd., Guangdong, China
Date of Manufacture: August 2012

9 8 7 6 5 4 3 2 1

This Is My Family

A FIRST LOOK AT SAME-SEX PARENTS

PAT THOMAS
ILLUSTRATED BY LESLEY HARKER

BARRON'S

In some families children may live with a mom and a dad. But that's not the only way to make a family.

In some families children may live with two dads or two moms.

7

A man who wants to be in a loving relationship
with another man is called gay.

A woman who wants to be
in a loving relationship with
another woman is called a lesbian.

There are gay men and lesbian women in every community. They work and teach and help others and make friends.

And sometimes they fall in love.

When any two adults love each other it is normal for them to want to live together and celebrate their love by making a family.

What about you?

Who are the people in your family? Do you know the difference between a loving relationship and a friendship?

Gay and lesbian parents
can't always make
a baby the way other
parents do.

Babies come to these parents in different ways.

They may bring children
with them from other relationships,
or they may choose to adopt a child.

What about you?

What do you know about your family?

Do you have brothers and sisters?

Same-sex parents love and protect and take care of their children just like all parents do.

They take you to school or to the doctor.

They teach you respect for others and the
difference between right and wrong.

They also do fun stuff too, like play
with you, cuddle with you,
and read with you.

16

They teach you how to do new things and give
you special treats and presents.

And they know how to cheer
you up when you are feeling sad.

Each of your parents brings special skills to your family. They each have different jobs and hobbies and things that interest them...

They each have some things they are good at...

...and some things they are not so good at!

Some people don't understand when they see a family with two moms or two dads. They may feel embarrassed or afraid, or think it's wrong for two men or two women to make a family.

What about you?

Has anyone ever been unkind about your family? What did they say? Did you talk to someone about it?

20

They may say unkind things to you and try to make you feel bad about your family.

Being mean to someone because they are different is a form of bullying. Bullies are often afraid of things that are different or that they don't understand.

If someone is mean to you about your family, you should always talk to your parents or your teacher about it.

They can help you understand that a loving family
is never bad or wrong and that the world is much
more interesting when we are not all the same.

There's more than one way to make a family.
Where you live, there are many different kinds
of families made from people of all shapes, colors,
ages, abilities, and sexes.

What about you?

How many different kinds of families do you know?

But there are some things that make all families the same.

Like the way they try to love and support one another.

Think of it this way.
The world and all the
people in it are like
a wonderful rainbow...

26

...your family adds another beautiful color to that rainbow for everyone to enjoy.

HOW TO USE THIS BOOK

You may be reading this book to your child simply because you want to explain more about your family, or you may be reading this book to them because they have been made to feel bad about their family being "different." This book provides several opportunities to stop and talk with your child about key issues. Before you begin, it's worth taking some time to examine your own feelings/beliefs about homosexuality, about the community where you live, your family values and the people you know, before talking to your child.

Celebrate diversity. Help your child understand there are many different kinds of families. Very young children are not naturally inclined to make judgments about family structure. They see family structure as a fact. While they may not comprehend the complexities of adult relationships—gay or straight—young children do understand love and affection. They know who is in their immediate family (mommy and daddy, mommy and mommy, daddy and daddy, just mommy or daddy, etc.). Build on this.

Use simple, direct language, and help the people in your family and community to do the same. Many people around you will feel shy about using the words "gay," "lesbian," "bisexual," or "transgender" fearing they may be taken as insults. Help your child to see these are not "bad" words but simply descriptions and statements of fact. Bringing these words out of the closet reduces their power to be used as weapons later on.

Educate those around you. As children get older they may face the same pressures and ridicule that kids from other minorities face. You may never be able to prevent this completely, but you can do some groundwork now. When opportunities present themselves talk to your child about prejudice—what it is, why it's wrong and how we deal with it. Engage teachers and caregivers by suggesting children's books that deal with these issues for the school library, talk to your child's teacher so they can help to educate others about your family structure.

Children are what we make them. Those who are raised in a nurturing environment where they feel loved, supported, and valued have the best chance of developing a healthy self-image. Youngsters who feel good about themselves and confident of their place in the world are less likely to be fearful or mistrustful of those who are different from them. Likewise, if you are respectful of all people, your children will follow the example.

At school, teachers may be constrained about what they can or cannot say about sexual orientation. Where school guidelines, and in some cases local laws, allow, encourage discussions about family diversity, reinforcing the idea that a family is "the circle of people who love you."

Schools are ideal places to reinforce the ideas of diversity and tolerance. Most of the time this is done indirectly, for instance by celebrating the holidays and festivals of diverse cultures, and teaching about the traditions and foods of different cultures. Where possible, teachers may wish to be more proactive. "Circle time" groups can open the door for discussions about important topics such as racism, prejudice, and bullying. Family tree projects are a good way to help children understand the diversity of families that exist.

Teachers should work with parents to ensure that anti-discrimination policies—both in theory and in practice—encompass sexual orientation.

BOOKS TO READ

For children

It's Okay To Be Different
Todd Parr
(Little, Brown Young Readers, 2009)

Mommy, Mama and ME
Leslea Newman and Carol Thompson
(Tricycle Press, 2009)

Daddy, Papa and ME
Leslea Newman and Carol Thompson
(Tricycle Press, 2009)

If I Had 100 Mummies
Vanda Carter
(Onlywomen Press Ltd, 2007)

My Two Grannies
Floella Benjamin and Margaret Chamberl
(Frances Lincoln Children's Books, 2009)

Heather Has Two Mommies
Leslea Newman and Diana Souza
(Alyson Books, 2000)

For adults

**Families Like Mine: Children of
Gay Parents Tell It Like It Is**
Abigail Garner
(Harper Paperbacks, 2005)

Gay Parenting
Shana Priwer and Dr. Cynthia Phillips
(New Horizon Press Publishers Inc., 2006)

RESOURCES FOR ADULTS

**Parents, Families, and Friends of Lesbians
and Gays (PFLAG)**
Operates in the US and UK and offers comprehensive
tips and support for gay and lesbian parents.
http://www.pflag.co.uk

The Human Rights Campaign Family Project
Serves as a comprehensive resource for gay, lesbian,
bisexual, and transgender families.
http://www.hrc.org

Pink Parents UK
A UK-wide organization of, by, and for lesbian,
gay, bisexual and transgender parents, parents-to-be
and their children.
www.pinkparents.org.uk

Family Equality Council (US)
Works to ensure that all families—especially those
with lesbian, gay, bisexual, and transgender parents—
are respected, loved, and celebrated.
http://www.familypride.org